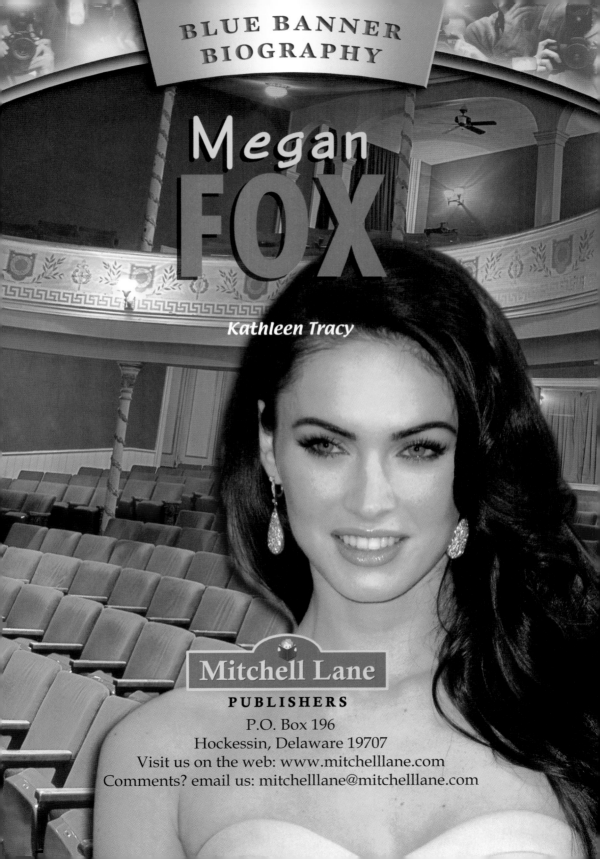

BLUE BANNER
BIOGRAPHY

Megan
FOX

Kathleen Tracy

Mitchell Lane

PUBLISHERS

P.O. Box 196
Hockessin, Delaware 19707
Visit us on the web: www.mitchelllane.com
Comments? email us: mitchelllane@mitchelllane.com

Mitchell Lane
PUBLISHERS

Printing   1   2   3   4   5   6   7   8   9

Blue Banner Biographies

Akon	Flo Rida	Megan Fox
Alicia Keys	Gwen Stefani	Miguel Tejada
Allen Iverson	Ice Cube	Missy Elliott
Ashanti	Ja Rule	Nancy Pelosi
Ashlee Simpson	Jamie Foxx	Natasha Bedingfield
Ashton Kutcher	Jay-Z	Orianthi
Avril Lavigne	Jennifer Lopez	Orlando Bloom
Beyoncé	Jessica Simpson	P. Diddy
Blake Lively	J. K. Rowling	Peyton Manning
Bow Wow	Joe Flacco	Pink
Brett Favre	John Legend	Queen Latifah
Britney Spears	Johnny Depp	Rihanna
Carrie Underwood	Justin Berfield	Robert Pattinson
Chris Brown	Justin Timberlake	Ron Howard
Chris Daughtry	Kanye West	Sean Kingston
Christina Aguilera	Kate Hudson	Selena
Christopher Paul Curtis	Keith Urban	Shakira
Ciara	Kelly Clarkson	Shia LaBeouf
Clay Aiken	Kenny Chesney	Shontelle Layne
Cole Hamels	Kristen Stewart	Soulja Boy Tell 'Em
Condoleezza Rice	Lady Gaga	Stephenie Meyer
Corbin Bleu	Lance Armstrong	Taylor Swift
Daniel Radcliffe	Leona Lewis	T.I.
David Ortiz	Lil Wayne	Timbaland
David Wright	Lindsay Lohan	Tim McGraw
Derek Jeter	Mariah Carey	Toby Keith
Drew Brees	Mario	Usher
Eminem	Mary J. Blige	Vanessa Anne Hudgens
Eve	Mary-Kate and Ashley Olsen	Zac Efron
Fergie		

Library of Congress Cataloging-in-Publication Data
Tracy, Kathleen.
  Megan Fox / by Kathleen Tracy.
    p. cm. — (Blue banner biographies)
  Includes bibliographical references and index.
  Includes filmography and webliography.
  ISBN 978-1-58415-912-4 (library bound)
  1. Fox, Megan, 1986– —Juvenile literature. 2. Actors—United States—Biography—Juvenile literature. I. Title.
PN2287.F6245T63 2010
791.4302'8092—dc22
  [B]
                                                    2010008945

PARENTS AND TEACHERS STRONGLY CAUTIONED: The story of Megan Fox's life may not be appropriate for younger readers.

ABOUT THE AUTHOR: Kathleen Tracy has been a journalist for over twenty years. Her writing has been featured in magazines including *The Toronto Star*'s "Star Week," *A&E Biography* magazine, *KidScreen*, and *TV Times*. She is also the author of over 85 books, including numerous books for Mitchell Lane Publishers, such as *The Fall of the Berlin Wall*; *Paul Cézanne*; *The Story of September 11, 2001*; *The Clinton View*; *We Visit Cuba*; *Johnny Depp*; *Mariah Carey*; *Orianthi*; and *Kelly Clarkson*. Tracy lives in the Los Angeles area with her two dogs and African Grey parrot.

Blue Banner Biography

After Transformers came out in 2007, Megan Fox went from virtually unknown to Hollywood's latest breakout star. At Spike TV's 2008 Guys Choice Awards, she won the Next Big Thing award.

Feeling the Heat

*G*rowing up, we are told it is wrong to lie and that it's important to tell the truth. And in general, that's true. But sometimes it's possible to be *too* honest, especially when you're a celebrity and your comments get published around the world. That's the lesson *Transformers* star Megan Fox learned the hard way.

In June 2009 while promoting *Transformers 2: Revenge of the Fallen* on the CBS *Early Show*, Fox admitted she wasn't completely sure what the movie was about. "I'm in the movie and I read the script and I watched the movie and I still didn't know what was happening," Fox joked. "So I think if you haven't read the script and you go and you see it and you understand it, you may be a genius. It's a movie for geniuses."

Megan also called the movie massive. "I don't know how you saw it in IMAX without having a brain aneurysm or at least a migraine headache!"

Some *Transformers* fans were upset because they felt she had dissed the movie. Rather than censor herself, Megan created even more controversy during an interview with

Wonderland Magazine. During that interview, Megan was asked what it was like working with *Transformers* director Michael Bay.

"When we make a Transformers movie . . . [Bay] has you do some really insane things insurance would never let you do."

"God, I really wish I could go loose on this one," Megan said. And then she did, comparing Bay to Napoleon. "He wants to create this insane, infamous mad-man reputation." Then she said the director was like Hitler on his sets, meaning he acted like a tyrant. "He's a nightmare to work for . . . Shia [LaBeouf] and I almost die when we make a *Transformers* movie. He has you do some really insane things that insurance would never let you do."

Even when she spoke highly of Bay, it sounded like an insult. "When you get him away from set, and he's not in director mode, I kind of really enjoy his personality because he's so awkward, so hopelessly awkward. He has no social skills at all. And it's endearing to watch him. He's vulnerable and fragile in real life and then on set he's a tyrant."

A few days later Michael Bay responded to the *Wall Street Journal*. "Well, that's Megan Fox for you," the director said. "She says some very ridiculous things because she's 23 years old and she still has a lot of growing to do. . . . Nobody in the world knew about Megan Fox until I found her and put her in *Transformers*."

Megan's comments prompted three *Transformers* crew members to write an open letter to Michael Bay fans and post it on the director's web site: "We are three crew members

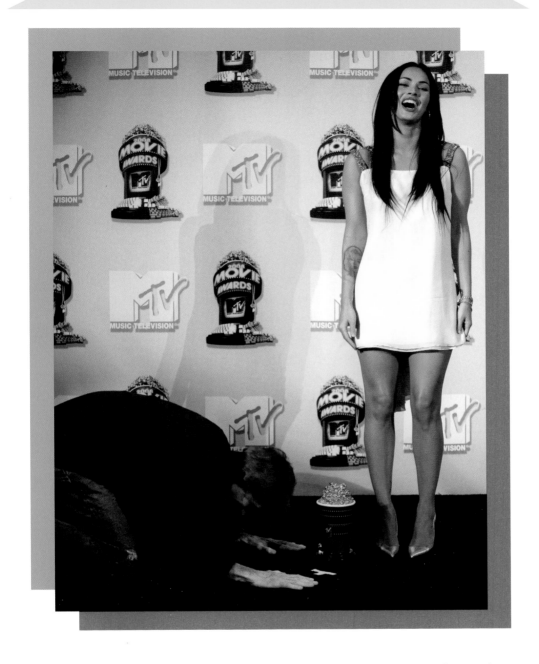

Transformers *director Michael Bay jokingly bows at Megan's feet at the 2008 MTV Awards where* Transformers *won Best Picture. A short while later, Bay and Fox would have a dispute over comments she made about his directing style.*

that have worked with Michael for the past ten years. Last week we read the terrible article with inflammatory, truly trashing quotes by Ms. Fox about Michael Bay. This letter is to set a few things straight. . . .

"She became one of the most Googled and oogled [sic] women on earth. . . . She was the next Angelina Jolie . . ."

"Michael found this shy, inexperienced girl, plucked her out of total obscurity thus giving her the biggest shot of any young actresses' [sic] life. . . . She became one of the most Googled and oogled [sic] women on earth. . . . She was the next Angelina Jolie, hooray! Wait a minute, two of us worked with Angelina—second thought—she's no Angelina. You see, Angelina is a professional . . ."

The letter went on to call Megan "dumb as a rock" and "thankless, classless, graceless [and] unfriendly."

When Megan heard about the letter, she acknowledged she sometimes spoke before she thought. "I've definitely said some things that I shouldn't say," she admitted to *The Telegraph*. "I sometimes forget how things will translate once they are in print."

Bay removed the crew letter from his web site in September and replaced it with a friendly note of his own. "I don't condone the crew letter to Megan. And I don't condone Megan's outlandish quotes. But her crazy quips are part of her crazy charm," he said. "The fact of the matter [is] I still love working with her, and I know we still get along. I even expect more crazy quotes from her on *Transformers 3*."

At the 2009 Scream Awards in Los Angeles, Megan Fox took home the trophy for Best Sci-Fi Actress. She took the opportunity to apologize to Bay for her remarks about him.

In October 2009, Megan won Best Sci-Fi Actress at the fourth annual Scream Awards. During her acceptance speech she also tried to make amends. "I don't usually do this, but I wanted to say something," she said. "There have been a lot of false reports about how I feel about this movie. I just want to be very clear that I've always felt I'm a very ordinary part of an extraordinary film. . . . The movie took me out of obscurity and gave me a career, and I'm completely grateful to everyone involved with this franchise."

It wasn't the first time Megan's candor had landed her in hot water. Long before she became nationally known, she was a rebel.

Fox appeared at New York's Olympus Fashion Week in September 2005. She says her time on the East Coast was lonely.

Rebel

Megan Denise Fox was born May 16, 1986, in Oak Ridge, Tennessee, and grew up in nearby Rockport. "It's like a semi-mountain town, very rural," she recalled to *GQ* magazine. "My dad used to hunt ducks and my mom would put them in the pot. We lived really modestly. We had very little money."

Megan's father, Franklin, was a parole officer who changed his surname from Foxx to Fox before Megan was born. Her mother, Darlene, worked many different jobs, including a stint as a county tourism director. Megan has one sibling, Kristi, who is four years older.

From the time she could walk and talk, Megan says she wanted to be an actress. She told the *Palm Beach Post* that Judy Garland in *The Wizard of Oz* was her inspiration.

"For a year after I saw that movie, Mom had to call me Dorothy. I had the red shoes. I wore the pigtails. I knew all her lines. Everything. I guess that's what started it."

Describing herself as obnoxiously outgoing, Megan put on shows in their living room. "I just always wanted everyone's attention to be focused on me."

Darlene told *Cosmopolitan* that her daughter knew what she wanted from the time she was small. "She was very determined and ambitious. She did everything—dance class, choir, plays."

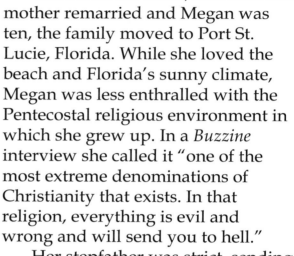

"You cannot be anything other than yourself, and you can't be untrue to yourself."

The Foxes divorced, and after her mother remarried and Megan was ten, the family moved to Port St. Lucie, Florida. While she loved the beach and Florida's sunny climate, Megan was less enthralled with the Pentecostal religious environment in which she grew up. In a *Buzzine* interview she called it "one of the most extreme denominations of Christianity that exists. In that religion, everything is evil and wrong and will send you to hell."

Her stepfather was strict, sending Megan to Morningside Academy, a Christian school, for her freshman and sophomore years. "They had right-wing conservative teachers teaching Bible class," she said in an *Esquire* interview. "They'd tell us how abortion was wrong, how evolution was wrong, how sex was wrong." She responded by "rebelling against everything that I was ever taught or told." Megan told David Letterman that as a teen, she was "sort of loudmouth and obnoxious. I was never really good with authority figures."

Not surprisingly, Megan disliked school. "I wasn't interested and I wasn't getting anything from it," she told *CosmoGirl*. "I've never been a big believer in formal education and I always knew what I wanted to do, which was be an actress — the education I was getting seemed irrelevant. So, I was sort of checked out on that part of it."

Instead of taking notes, she spent a lot of time drawing, a passion that led to an interest in anime. "When I was twelve, Adult Swim on Cartoon Network started, and they had a lot of anime cartoons on, like *Cowboy Bebop* and *InuYasha*. I'd also been a fan of graphic novels, so it's that kind of art as well as Japanime art that I'm in love with."

Her artistic interests helped Megan cope with feeling like an outcast. "I was not, ever for a second, popular," she told *Buzzine*. "I mean, never. Everyone hated me," she claims — especially other girls. "I have a very aggressive personality, and girls didn't like me for that. I've had only one great girlfriend my whole life."

Looking back, Megan told *CosmoGirl*, the experience taught her an important lesson. "You cannot be anything other than yourself, and you can't be untrue to yourself. You can't just go with whatever clique you're hanging out with, and you can't be swayed by what your friends want to do."

Unfortunately, Megan wasn't swayed by what her parents wanted, either. When Megan was eleven, she attended a Bible camp. In an interview with *Blender*, she sarcastically called the experience "awesome. You sing songs about Jesus and then you do arts and crafts about Jesus." Of course, Megan found more to do, such as sneaking out "to meet the first boy I ever had a crush on." As she got older, she continued to be a free spirit.

"I was always wearing the smallest clothes I could find. I would go to the mall . . . in a short, short skirt and a giant wedge heel. That's what you do when you're a teenage girl in a small town." Megan admits that when she was fourteen, she would steal her mom's car, "because I was always grounded and she would never drive me anywhere."

Megan's teenage rebelliousness would soon give way to more constructive and mature pursuits.

Heading West

At an age when most teenagers are worried about getting their homework done, Megan had her sights set on a performing career. By that time, she had started making headway as a performer. In 1999, when she was thirteen, Megan won some awards at the American Modeling and Talent Convention in Hilton Head Island, South Carolina. She also appeared in local theater, including a 2000 production of *Godspell* at Stuart's Lyric Theatre. In 2001, she made her screen debut as a spoiled heiress in *Holiday in the Sun*, a direct-to-video film starring the Olsen twins.

Not every "performing" job was as fun. "I worked at a Tropical Smoothie in Florida," she told *Blender*. "I would sometimes have to go out by the street in a gigantic banana costume and dance to try to get customers to come in." The costume had a big hole cut out so that everyone could see her face. "My friends from school would drive back and forth and yell all kinds of awesome obscenities at me."

When she was fifteen, she was cast as an extra on the film *Bad Boys II*, shot in Delray Beach—and directed by Michael Bay. She played a club kid dancing under a waterfall wearing a stars-and-stripes bikini and a cowboy hat. Despite her young age, Megan was comfortable in her sexy role. "I thought it was awesome. I was going to a Christian high school and I wasn't a feminist yet. I hadn't sat back and analyzed society yet. I was fifteen! I just did what I was told to do." She also was happy just to be out of school. "And if you allow them to put water on you, you get paid extra."

> *"I would have to go out by the street in a giant banana costume and dance to try to get customers to come in."*

Performing did not help her popularity, though. In an interview with the *Palm Beach Post* in 2001, Megan noted, "I think a lot of times people — especially girls my age — when they hear I [act], they think I'm going to be self-absorbed, conceited, and I'm not that way at all. I'm not rude. I'm not a scary person. I am actually pretty nice."

She was also determined. While her sister, Kristi, would go on to become an elementary school teacher in Port St. Lucie, Megan's dreams were too big for Florida. After appearing in the mystery telenovela *Ocean Ave.* in 2002, which was taped in Miami, Megan convinced her mother to take her to Los Angeles.

With the move, she would be leaving behind her boyfriend of three years, Ben Leahy. "When Megan left it was heartbreaking," he told *News of the World*. "We had been inseparable for three years and then suddenly we lived thousands of miles apart. I'll never forget the day I waved her off, she clung to me and cried her heart out. She begged and begged me to go with her and said she had even packed

Fox (center) costarred with Lindsay Lohan in Confessions of a Teenage Drama Queen, *playing her high school rival. Her cohorts were played by Ashley Leggat (left) and Barbara Mamabolo.*

some of my stuff with her so I would not have to pack so much if I decided to go out."

Megan and her mother lived in a furnished apartment a few blocks from Warner Brothers Studios in Burbank. It wasn't long before she got her first L.A. job in *Confessions of a Teenage Drama Queen*, which starred Lindsay Lohan.

When Megan turned eighteen in May 2004, Darlene returned to Florida, and Megan stayed in L.A. She admits the first year of living on her own was a reckless one. She made friends and went through a partying phase and found herself in a strange situation she chooses not to elaborate on. What she will say is, "I was just careless."

She survived the experience and found new ways to express herself, such as through tattoos. It was also clear that she and Ben had drifted apart. They lived vastly different lives and had different goals. He finally broke off their relationship after he learned Megan was spending time with actor David Gallagher, best known for his role on *7th Heaven*.

Megan's first boyfriend after moving to Hollywood was actor David Gallagher. Their relationship was short-lived, and soon after they broke up, Megan moved to New York to work on the sitcom Hope & Faith.

As much as she enjoyed going out with friends in Los Angeles, Fox found New York isolating and lonely. Other than publicity functions, she says she rarely left her small apartment.

Megan and Gallagher dated for several months, and Megan says she was in love—but that relationship did not last, either.

In 2004, Megan replaced Nicole Paggi on the ABC sitcom *Hope & Faith*. Paggi was let go after it was reported she was twenty-seven years old but playing a teenager. The sitcom was taped in New York, and while working there she lived in a small apartment on the Lower East Side. She was miserable. She told writer Mark Kirby that she had no friends and never went out. "I was really isolated."

Megan was on the series for a year and a half until it was canceled. She moved back to L.A. full time and continued going on auditions, waiting for her breakout role. It didn't take long. Within a year, Megan would be world famous.

Transformation

*I*n the 2007 film *Transformers*, Megan played Mikaela Banes, Shia LaBeouf's onscreen love interest and partner in robot-fighting crime. The movie grossed over $700 million worldwide and made Megan an international star. The film also opened Hollywood doors.

"I've been able to be a part of some films that I don't really feel like I deserved to have been a part of and that's due greatly, if not solely, to the success of *Transformers*," she acknowledged to *Movies Online*. "Actors don't generally get those opportunities and, for me to have that, is a huge blessing."

The movie gave Megan enough financial security for her—and her six dogs—to move into a house with a pool in Hollywood Hills. She says when she got her first big paycheck, she paid her rent a year in advance—then bought a $600 pair of high heels. "All I knew up to that point was Skechers, and I think the most I had ever paid for a pair of shoes was $30," she told *CosmoGirl*. "That was a really big deal for me, and I have to admit that since then I've gone

The first extravagant present Fox ever bought herself was an expensive pair of shoes. She admits she's become a shoe-a-holic, especially for high heels.

crazy with the shoe thing. That's where I spend my money, and it's really bad."

At first, it seemed that Megan was reveling in her newfound fame. She told *Blender* that even though she was on the good guys' side in the movie, in real life she'd side with the bad *Transformers*. "I'm always forced to behave and be nice to people, so being bad is very appealing."

The thrill of being a celebrity soon gave way to unhappiness. "I grew up craving the spotlight and once it happened I immediately recoiled," she said. "Up until the very moment it happened I was really outgoing. Now I'm really introverted. I thought that I would love it, that this was the kind of life I wanted, that everyone wanted. And it's not all that it seems."

Megan noted that while growing up, the idea of being famous seemed glamorous. "As a child you think everyone who's famous is very wealthy and very powerful. I felt like, once I achieved that success then all of my internal issues would be solved and I would be this really confident person. And I'm not."

She described her insecurity as a feeling of not being acceptable. "I think that has something to do with my parents' divorce and not seeing my dad and always feeling rejected. You don't ever really get past that."

What made her insecurities worse was the idea that her success was largely based on her looks, not her acting ability. So, just as she did as a teenager, Megan rebelled. She started dressing like a tomboy and wore clothes that were too big for her.

At the time, Megan was preparing to star in the movie *Jennifer's Body*, a dark comedy about a high-school girl who is possessed by a demon and needs to eat the flesh of boys to stay alive. Paralyzingly unhappy, she lost so much weight that her hair started falling out. "I was depressed," she admits.

When she first became famous, Fox says she enjoyed the attention from fans and the media. But after a while she grew tired of being constantly in the spotlight. She also realized she wanted to be known for her work more than for her looks.

Although she has described herself as shy, Megan is outgoing with fans and takes time to sign autographs whenever possible.

Megan eventually snapped out of her depression and now has a healthier perspective. "All this opportunity has fallen in my lap that I'm grateful for," she told writer Alex Bilmes. "I feel like I'm growing out of that struggle I was going through to push away all the attention." Megan said she realized it was time to be appreciative. "Instead of fighting this I should be rejoicing that my only job is to get up, take a shower, do my hair and look attractive. I was being a brat. So I stopped."

What she can control is her image. While the media may play her up as a sex symbol, there are lines she says she will not cross, such as appearing topless in a movie. "When you become a celebrity, the world owns you and your image. The only thing still private and still mine is my actual physical body. It's literally all I have left that is my own."

With her insecurities under control, Megan was determined to prove she was more than an action-movie celebrity; she was ready to prove she was also an actress.

Learning Curve

*E*ven after the controversy with Michael Bay was over, Megan seemed disappointed people had been so quick to attack her. "I know that the things they said about me in the crew letter were not true. . . . I was waiting for someone to defend me, to say, 'That's not accurate,' but nobody did. I think it's because I'm a girl. They left me out there to be bludgeoned to death."

Megan was also frustrated at being misinterpreted. "When I do interviews, I say things that I think are hysterical," she told the *New York Times Magazine*. "But because we live in a world of sound bites, you're not allowed to have a sense of humor. Sarcasm doesn't translate in print at all. And neither does self-deprecating humor."

The second *Transformers* film, *Revenge of the Fallen*, was even more successful at the box office, earning in excess of $800 million worldwide. Ironically, Megan didn't see the movie until its London premiere. "I usually don't watch myself," she explained to *Movies Online*. "I don't watch playback. I don't look at still photos. I have a phobia of it."

In the first two Transformers *movies, Fox plays robot-fighting Mikaela Banes. She described the working conditions as difficult but said she was grateful for all the opportunities the films gave her.*

But once she saw the film, she admitted she was "really, really pleasantly surprised."

Even after this success, Megan still felt as if she was mostly window dressing. "If I really buckle down, I think one day I could be a very good actress. But so far, I haven't done anything yet." She believes that her openness and shoot-from-the-hip personality have saved her from being dismissed as eye candy.

"*Transformers* made $700 million and that opened a door to introduce this 'new girl' and I happened to be such an outrageous personality that people wanted to start writing about me because it was deemed controversial," she mused in *Entertainment Weekly.* "I think if I had been a typical Hollywood actress and said all the right things and had I been a publicity android, it wouldn't have escalated to this level."

Part of the media interest in Megan centered on her five-year relationship with Brian Austin Green, best known for his years on the 1990s' series *Beverly Hills 90210.* They began dating when Megan was eighteen and Green was thirty-one. The couple broke up in late 2009, and Megan found the experience wrenching.

"Whether or not he is currently my boyfriend or we are romantically involved, he's always going to be a really good friend of mine," Megan was quoted in *Contact Music.* "We had a very serious relationship . . . for five years and that doesn't just go away." While she doesn't believe her fame caused the breakup, she acknowledged her career may have. "The odd hours we keep and the different locations . . . I'm all over the place all the time. That's hard."

> *"Because no one knows me yet everyone knows me. It's a really bizarre feeling; kind of other-worldly."*

Megan continues to struggle with the isolation caused by celebrity. "There's a really overwhelming sense of loneliness," she described to writer Alex Bilmes. "Because no one knows me yet everyone knows me. It's a really bizarre feeling; kind of otherworldly." She noted to *Buzzine,* "I just don't necessarily see myself the way that the media portrays me," and when she looks in the mirror she just sees "a girl. Because my face is my face, and how I look is how I look, and

Fox has developed a fondness for tattoos. Among others, she has the face of Marilyn Monroe on her right forearm, tribal waves on her left wrist, and a quote from Shakespeare's King Lear on her right shoulder blade.

I can't really do anything about that, but I can constantly progress and grow as a person."

She took another step in May 2010 to allow for growth: she bowed out of *Transformers 3*. While Fox claimed it was her decision to leave, others wondered whether she was asked to go because of her fallout with Bay. The studio's story said that they wanted to give LaBeouf's character a new love interest.

Through it all, Megan has stayed true to her outspoken self. "I feel like most people in this business aim to make an image that is really very politically correct, and very android-like . . . [but] we're all human. We all do horrible things and great things. I would rather have an image that is wild and promiscuous than to go out of my way to be proper all of the time."

Somehow, it seems unlikely Megan will ever be fully bound by etiquette or convention.

> "I feel like most people in this business aim to make an image that is . . . very android-like . . . [but] we're all human."

1986   Born May 16 in Oak Ridge, Tennessee

1996   Moves to Port St. Lucie, Florida

1998   Becomes fan of anime on Adult Swim

1999   Competes in American Modeling and Talent
        Convention

2000   Appears in stage production of *Godspell*

2001   Makes screen debut in *Holiday in the Sun;* works at
        local smoothie store

2002   Appears in *Ocean Ave.*

2003   Appears as an extra in *Bad Boys II*, directed by Michael
        Bay; begins dating David Gallagher; is cast in
        Confessions of a Teenage Drama Queen, starring Lindsay
        Lohan

2004   Joins ABC sitcom *Hope & Faith*

2007   *Transformers* is released

2008   Appears in *How to Lose Friends & Alienate People*

2009   Wins Teen Choice Award for *Transformers: Revenge of
        the Fallen;* stars in *Jennifer's Body;* wins Scream Award
        for Best Sci-Fi Actress; breaks up with longtime
        boyfriend Brian Austin Green

2010   Begins filming *Passion Play;* leaves *Transformers*
        franchise; *Jonah Hex* is released

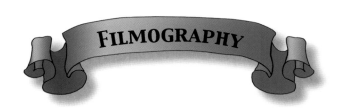

FILMOGRAPHY

2010   *Shrek Forever After*

Passion Play

Jonah Hex

2009   *Jennifer's Body*

Transformers: Revenge of the Fallen

2008   *How to Lose Friends & Alienate People*

Whore

2007   *Transformers*

2004   *Confessions of a Teenage Drama Queen*

Hope & Faith (TV series)

Two and a Half Men (TV series guest spot)

The Help (TV series)

Crimes of Fashion (TV)

2003   *Bad Boys II*

What I Like About You (TV series guest spot)

2002   *Ocean Ave.* (TV series)

2001   *Holiday in the Sun*

FURTHER READING

Books

While there are no other young adult books about Megan Fox, you may enjoy these other Blue Banner Biographies from Mitchell Lane Publishers:

Mattern, Joanne. *Blake Lively*. Hockessin, DE: Mitchell Lane Publishers, 2011.

Orr, Tamra. *Shia LaBeouf*. Hockessin, DE: Mitchell Lane Publishers, 2011.

Works Consulted

Bilmes, Alex. "Megan Fox: Exclusive Interview and Photos." *GQ*, July 2009.
    http://www.gq-magazine.co.uk/gq-daily-news/articles/090601-alex-bilmes-megan-fox.aspx

Caplan, David, and Jennifer Garcia. "Megan Fox: It Was My Decision to Leave Transformers." *People*, May 19, 2010.
    http://www.people.com/people/article/0,,20386636,00.html?xid=rss-fullcontent

CBS News, "Megan Fox Heats Up Big Screen," June 30, 2009.
    http://www.cbsnews.com/stories/2009/06/30/earlyshow/leisure/celebspot/main5125337.shtml

Dickinson, Georgina. " 'I Turned Megan Fox Lesbian.' " *News of the World*, September 28, 2008.
    http://www.newsoftheworld.co.uk/showbiz/article34662.ece

Hiscock, John. "Megan Fox: Interview for *Jennifer's Body*," *Daily Telegraph*, October 23, 2009.
    http://www.telegraph.co.uk/culture/film/6398707/Megan-Fox-interview-on-Jennifers-Body.html

Itier, Emmanuel. "Megan Fox Interview," *Buzzine*, September 2009.
    http://www.buzzine.com/2009/09/megan-fox-interview/

Katz, David. "Good Morning, Megan." *Esquire*, June 1, 2009.
    http://www.highbeam.com/doc/1G1-200116765.html

Kirby, Mark. "Megan Fox Was a Teenage Lesbian!" *GQ*, September 2008.
http://www.gq.com/women/photos/200809/actress-model-transformers-sexiest-woman-in-the-world

"Megan Fox." *CosmoGirl*, June/July 2009.
http://www.cosmogirl.com/entertainment/celeb-qa/megan-fox-qa

Nashawaty, Chris. " 'Fallen' Angel" *Entertainment Weekly*, June 10, 2009.
http://www.ew.com/ew/article/0,,20246950_20263258_20284375,00.html

Prato, Alison. "The Devil in Megan Fox." *Cosmopolitan*, October 2009. http://www.highbeam.com/doc/1G1-210724385.html

Roberts, Sheila. "Megan Fox Interview, *Revenge of the Fallen*." Movies Online, n.d.
http://www.moviesonline.ca/movienews_16891.html

Yarm, Mark. "Transformers Star Megan Fox Will Pee in Your Pool." *Blender*, June 27, 2007.
http://www.blender.com/guide/68768/interview-itransformersi-star-megan-fox-will-pee-in-your-pool.html

On the Internet

MSN Movies: Megan Fox
http://movies.msn.com/celebrities/celebrity/megan-fox/

Transformers: Revenge of the Fallen
http://www.transformersmovie.com/

PHOTO CREDITS: Cover—Steve Granitz/WireImage; p. 4—Frank Micelotta/Getty Images; p. 7—AP Photo/Chris Pizzello; p. 8—M. Brown/Getty Images; p. 10—Katy Winn/Getty Images; pp. 16, 24—ES/Globe Photos, Inc.; p. 17—Jon Kopaloff/Getty Images; p. 18—Andrea Renault/Globe Photos, Inc.; p. 20—Mark Sullivan/WireImage; p. 21—Sipa via AP Images; p. 22—Jordan Strauss/WireImage; p. 26—Michael Germana/Globe Photos, Inc. Every effort has been made to locate all copyright holders of material used in this book. If any errors or omissions have occurred, corrections will be made in future editions of this book.

INDEX

11-1-11

DATE DUE		
DE 22		